A 31 Day Devotional

by Patrick Malcolm

All rights reserved. Except as permitted under the U.S. Copyright Act of 1976, no part of this publication may be reproduced, distributed, or transmitted in any form or by any means, or stored in a database or retrieval system, without the prior written permission of the publisher, except for a reviewer, who may quote excerpts from the book for a review. For permission, please direct your written request to the publisher e-mail address provided below:

Makatree1@gmail.com

Printed in the United State of America
Copyright© 2013 by Peje-Patrick Malcolm Publishing
ISBN No.: 978-0-9890237-0-2

Scriptures are taken from the Holy Bible, King James Version

Interior and Exterior Graphic Design
provided by Irene Michel
illestr8tor@gmail.com

This is a special gift for you because you are a special person. Please accept this book as a token of my affection. May you live life knowing The Lmit Is When You Say Stop.™

❖TO

❖FROM

❖DATE

Acknowledgement

First and foremost, I want to thank God for His everlasting love, guidance and protection in my life since childhood. I thank God for the gift of discernment, patience, perserverance and the desire to reach out and help others. Without the guidance and protection of the Holy Spirit, I could have never reached and experienced the love and fulfillment I do today.

Also, I want to thank my loving family for their love, support and encouragement through the development of this book: To my Graphic Artist may God continue to bless you for your genuine heart, hard work, creativity and tireless nights until the completion of this book, you are heaven sent. To my friends, that are like family, including my Facebook/Twitter family, thank you for your love and encouragement as I worked endlessly to share my daily devotions with all of you; your feedback and support will never be forgotten.

If I have forgotten anyone, forgive me in advance. For in my heart, you all remain special and dear to me, thanks for having faith in me and this book. Also, special Thanks to the Checmate™ App Staff.

Insight

How far can the naked eye see? Depends on how well your vision is you might think. However, when you have faith, a dream and belief in yourself, your vision goes beyond your physical vision; you can see with the eyes of your heart.

'The Limit Is When You Say Stop™' is an inspirational diary of devotions and a testament written for those who wish to experience a transformation of self, body and mind amidst life's challenges. Overcoming such challenges of life does not happen overnight, but dedicating 31 days for change, focus and reflection is a good start. This book is written with the hope that anyone who gets a chance to read it will open their eyes to dreams, and reflect on the new possibilities of becoming a stronger and happier individual.

Dedication

This book is dedicated to all those who believed in me and supported me through the development of this book. Many were skeptical, which is ok, because God is faithful even still and with Him all things are possible. Therefore, this book has been written for all those who are ready to look for the positive in life and make a difference to those around them.

Much Love

A Prayer

Dear God,
Open my eyes so I can see the things I cannot see.
Open my ears so I can hear the things I cannot hear. Father,
I've been broken, I've been hurt, I've been wronged, and now I'm
humbled. So father, I come to you as an empty vessel needing to be
filled. Give me strength, understanding, patience, love, kindness,
forgiveness and temperance. More so Lord, give me the zeal of
understanding so I can know right from wrong. More importantly,
give me the understanding to hear and recognize your voice. As I
embark on this journey for the next 31 days, please open my mind to
your ways so that I may learn to listen, speak, feel, think and act as
you would. So that I may know in my heart all things are possible
with you Lord, and that The Limit Is When You Say Stop! ™

Respectfully,

Yours

Table of Contents

Day 1	Today is A New Day	01
Day 2	Forgiveness	07
Day 3	Acceptance	13
Day 4	Letting Go	19
Day 5	Finding Inner Peace	27
Day 6	You are Not Your Mistakes	35
Day 7	Agree to Disagree	43
Day 8	Distance Judging	49
Day 9	It's My Time	55
Day 10	Our Relationship	61
Day 11	Imaginary Wall	69
Day 12	A Word	77
Day 13	Self-Image	83
Day 14	Emotional Bondage	91
Day 15	Too Good to be True	99
Day 16	Angels in the Dark	107
Day 17	Two of a Kind	115
Day 18	Our Independence	123
Day 19	What About Me?	129
Day 20	Your Efforts	137
Day 21	The Ladder of Life	145
Day 22	Heart of a Champion	151
Day 23	Thank You	157
Day 24	Success Pill	165
Day 25	Greed and Pride	171
Day 26	Quitting	179
Day 27	Hidden Talents	185
Day 28	Aging Gracefully	193
Day 29	One Moment	199
Day 30	Student to Teacher	205
Day 31	A Dying Wish	211

The Limit Is When You Say Stop™

Day One

Today Is A New Day

22: It is of the LORD's mercies that we are not consumed, because his compassions fail not. 23: They are new every morning: great is thy faithfulness. 24: The Lord is my portion, saith my soul; therefore will I hope in him.
Lamentations 3:22-24

Today is a new day to start over and to celebrate the first day of the rest of your life. Knowing that you have one more chance to right your wrongs of yesterday and to behold the maturity you are gaining from life's experiences. In life, there will be bright days and dark days, therefore, instead of focusing on the dark days, find it in your heart to recreate the bright days. In the end, you will look back and see that it was just a learning experience, knowing that good choices comes from experience and experience comes from bad and good choices. You can learn from the child in the womb and the man in the tomb, so keep an open mind as you go through life. God will never give you more than you can bare, so stand tall and watch God work in your life. He did it before and He will do it again.

Today's Focus

- ❖ Focus on the blessings you have today and do not look at what you do not have. When you appreciate the little things in life, you will open the doors for bigger things.
- ❖ Today is a new day, the mistakes of yesterday are now an experience, learn from your mistakes and move on.
- ❖ Learn from yesterday's mistakes but don't dwell on them, they do not define who you are. *You Define Who You Are.*

Reflection

❖How do you define who you are?
❖Do you believe others see you this way?

Reflection

- How do you define who you are?
- Do you believe others see you this way?

Today Is A New Day

The Limit Is When You Say Stop™

Forgiveness

And be ye kind one to another, tenderhearted, forgiving one another, even as God for Christ's sake hath forgiven you. Ephesians 4:32

Often times, we make mistakes and then ask for forgiveness. We hope that the offended individual will understand our explanation for our actions and find it in his or her heart to forgive us. On the other hand, when we are offended by someone else's mistakes, we sometimes hold it against them because we know they were wrong and no matter what explanation they give us, it still doesn't change the fact they were wrong. We sometimes put the individual through mental torture by ignoring their apology and having them do things that we wouldn't do ourselves, so they can make up for their wrongs.

Ask yourself the next time you are planning on letting someone pay for their wrongs, "Would I want someone to put me through this?" Most mistakes are what they are, MISTAKES! When you stay mad at someone, you are missing out on fun times with that individual and eventually you will be more sad than happy, especially if the person dies and you are still angry at them. Life is short, so have fun! Be quick to forgive and slow to anger, God forgives us, so we should forgive others.

Today's Focus

- ❖ The Golden Rule: Treat others as you would have them treat you.
- ❖ Holding on to pain, mistakes, and offences done by others, only hardens your heart and prevents you from moving forward in life.
- ❖ Be quick to forgive, because no one is perfect.

Reflection

- What does it gain you to hold on to pain and be unforgiving?
- Have you ever mistakenly offended someone then asked for forgiveness?
- How does it feel when you ask for forgiveness?
- How does it feel when you are forgiven versus when you are not forgiven?

Reflection

- What does it gain you to hold on to pain and be unforgiving?
- Have you ever mistakenly offended someone then asked for forgiveness?
- How does it feel when you ask for forgiveness?
- How does it feel when you are forgiven versus when you are not forgiven?

The Limit Is When You Say Stop™

Acceptance

Let us therefore follow after the things which make for peace, and things wherewith one may edify another.
Romans 14:19

The feeling of being accepted is very fulfilling. The danger lies when you lose yourself to pressure from your peers. Often times, an individual will do or say whatever it takes to be in a particular circle/group, even if it means ignoring the morals and ethical values they were taught. Eventually, they realize that being someone other than themselves, will leave them feeling betrayed, empty and alone simply because they just can't keep up with the pace that pressure requires. For example; if it's purchasing a car, they won't get the one they like, instead, they'll get the one that the people in their circle like. This goes for almost every decision they'll ever have to make.

Why would you want to sacrifice your happiness to please someone else? Being true to yourself will bring you joy and satisfaction. Take time to get to know who you are and be honest in your choices. Always remember, it is easy to forget a lie, but in the end the truth will remain. BE TRUE TO YOURSELF.

Today's Focus

- ❖ Material items will not gain you true acceptance.
- ❖ Living your life based on the approval of others, will rob you of the person God made you to be.
- ❖ Never sacrifice your morals and ethics for anyone's acceptance.
- ❖ True self-acceptance comes from you loving and accepting who you are.

Reflection

- Do you find yourself trying to please everyone, while going against your morals and ethics?
- Are you struggling with who you are, versus who you want to be?
- Do you like who you see when you look in the mirror?

Acceptance

Reflection

- Do you find yourself trying to please everyone, while going against your morals and ethics?
- Are you struggling with who you are, versus who you want to be?
- Do you like who you see when you look in the mirror?

Acceptance

The Limit Is When You Say Stop™

Day Four

Letting Go

14: For if ye forgive men their trespasses, your heavenly Father will also forgive you. 15: But if ye forgive not men their trespasses, neither will your Father forgive your trespasses. Matthew 6:14-15

We sometimes make decisions based on our past experiences. It is very important that we don't hold on to the negatives, instead, learn from them. Holding on to the negatives, will sometimes prevent us from experiencing success and happiness. As in our relationships with others, many times individuals hold a certain group of people responsible for the actions of one person from that group, which is unfair. Each person is responsible for their own actions, regardless of the source of influence.

In the event of losing a loved one, it may seem as if life will never be the same, and in some ways it won't, because the loss of someone changes the dynamics of families and friendships. However, we must continue with our lives and try to focus on the great times we spent with that individual, knowing that they are in a better place now. Worrying and being stressed out will not bring you any comfort, instead, it will consume any little joy you have left in you. So get up, get moving and instead of crying and being down, take time to thank God for blessing you with their unforgettable memory.

Your thoughts of life will dictate your process of actions, therefore, having a positive outlook on life will help you to move forward, while accomplishing your goals.

Today's Focus

- ❖ The mistake made by an individual doesn't really define who they are.
- ❖ Give up the dead weight of negativity and negative people, and you will prosper and be happier.
- ❖ Holding on to the past will only rob you of your future.
- ❖ Let go and let God.

Reflection

- ❖Who is in control of your happiness?
- ❖Do you find yourself blaming one particular group of people for one person's mistake?
- ❖What are you gaining from holding on to the past?

Reflection

❖Who is in control of your happiness?
❖Do you find yourself blaming one particular group of people for one person's mistake?
❖What are you gaining from holding on to the past?

Letting Go

Reflection

- Who is in control of your happiness?
- Do you find yourself blaming one particular group of people for one person's mistake?
- What are you gaining from holding on to the past?

The Limit Is When You Say Stop™

The Limit Is When You Say Stop™

Finding Inner Peace

Pleasant words are as an honeycomb, sweet to the soul, and health to the bones. Proverbs 16:24

As technology advances, our lives are interrupted with the constant learning of new things. However, this constant interruption facilitates our stress. In addition, we spend so much time thinking of things from the past that we cannot change and worrying about the future, which may never happen. The folks who worked in the World Trade Center buildings during the 9/11 attacks were all planning for future events and in a flash they were all gone. It's very important to plan for tomorrow, but we should never let the plans of tomorrow cast a dark cloud on living today.

Finding inner peace, in a fast paced world such as ours, takes focus and dedication. Simplifying our lives, accepting the things we cannot change and helping others, are three basic ways to finding inner peace. One of the most fulfilling feelings one could ever experience, is the feeling of gratitude received from helping someone. Let's face it, life is unpredictable. We often find ourselves in situations that seem so serious, therefore, the natural instinct for us is to worry, get depressed and think of the worst case scenerio. Yet, no matter how stressful the situation, you have to *remain calm*, *stay focused* and *think positive*, because worrying will not provide a solution. Inner peace is not granted, it is found and *only you* can control *your* feelings.

Today's Focus

- ❖ Treat yourself occasionally.
- ❖ Don't be afraid to spend time alone.
- ❖ Avoid distractions; anything that can separate you from quality time with your family such as, cell phones at the dinner table.
- ❖ Help others and make someone smile each day. Over time, you will be a joy to others and you will be appreciated more.
- ❖ Make time each day to pray and read the word of God.

Reflection

- What clutter gets in the way of your peace? Co-workers? Gossip? Insecurity? Fear?
- Do you find yourself thinking about what others think and feel about you?... If so, STOP IT!
- When was the last time you spoke with God?

Reflection

- ❖ What clutter gets in the way of your peace? Co-workers? Gossip? Insecurity? Fear?
- ❖ Do you find yourself thinking about what others think and feel about you?... If so, STOP IT!
- ❖ When was the last time you spoke with God?

Reflection

- What clutter gets in the way of your peace? Co-workers? Gossip? Insecurity? Fear?
- Do you find yourself thinking about what others think and feel about you?... If so, STOP IT!
- When was the last time you spoke with God?

The Limit Is When You Say Stop™

Day Six

You Are Not Your Mistakes

Confess your faults one to another, and pray one for another, that ye may be healed. The effectual fervent prayer of a righteous man availeth much. James 5:16

Mistakes are made everyday by everyone. It could be as simple as stepping into the shower before adjusting the water's temperature, to mistakes that are irreparable, such as serious injuries or death. Mistakes are what they are, 'Mistakes!' However, some mistakes, such as saying a curse word in front of someone, like your pastor, or maybe one of your peers that you look up to, can sometimes cause them to see or think of you differently due to the words you used or the things you did. It is so easy for some people to point out another person's mistake, but when the shoe is on the other foot, those people want compassion and understanding.

No matter how good of a person you are, you will always be known for your last mistake, because we live in a world where the negative dominates. Therefore, many folks enjoy tearing each other down, especially when your life is where they wish their life to be. You should never let anyone put a mark on you, because of a past mistake. Although, your mistake maybe exposed, theirs may be hidden for the time being. Knowing who you are and accepting your mistakes, while surrounding yourself with people who support and love you, will help you to maintain the person you are and are trying to become. No one is perfect, today is for you and tomorrow is for them. So keep the faith, stand strong and watch God light your path.

Today's Focus

- ❖ There will be mistakes made everyday because no one is perfect.
- ❖ When mistakes are made, be sure to get the full story before pointing fingers.
- ❖ Avoid the people who constantly remind you of your mistakes.
- ❖ If you know that you are wrong, be mature and admit your mistakes.

Reflection

- ❖ Have you ever made a mistake?
- ❖ Do you point fingers without having all the facts?
- ❖ Do you constantly remind someone of their mistakes?
- ❖ How are you at owning up to your mistakes?

Reflection

❖Have you ever made a mistake?
❖Do you point fingers without having all the facts?
❖Do you constantly remind someone of their mistakes?
❖How are you at owning up to your mistakes?

You Are Not Your Mistakes

Reflection

- Have you ever made a mistake?
- Do you point fingers without having all the facts?
- Do you constantly remind someone of their mistakes?
- How are you at owning up to your mistakes?

The Limit Is When You Say Stop™

Agree to Disagree

Grudge not one against another, brethren, lest ye be condemned: behold, the judge standeth before the door.
James 5:9

Let's face it! We all come from different backgrounds. Therefore, our views and ethical values may vary. This sometimes causes us to have disagreements with our peers. However, when personal and disrespectful comments are made, the dynamics of the discussion will change for the worse. At such point, any possible mutual understanding will go out the door and the gloves will come off, now making what was meant to be a civilized discussion an all out brawl.

Many people come from homes where the things one would consider normal, is foreign to them. Which make us all at some point stop and ask ourselves, "Is this for real?" Sorry to say, but, "Yes." Some people will surprise you when they express their views during certain discussions, because we were taught differently, and so our beliefs vary. So the next time you are tempted to get angry at someone for not sharing or agreeing with your views during a discussion, remember to first get an understanding of the person's background or just agree to disagree.

Today's Focus

- ❖ Based on our backgrounds, our views will vary.
- ❖ Avoid making disrespectful comments during discussions and disagreements.
- ❖ You are what you were taught and believe.
- ❖ It's ok to agree to disagree.

Reflection

- Do you believe that a person's background is a reflection of their outlook on life?
- Have you ever made a disrespectful comment during a disagreement?
- Do you agree that you are what you were taught and believe?

Reflection

- Do you believe that a person's background is a reflection of their outlook on life?
- Have you ever made a disrespectful comment during a disagreement?
- Do you agree that you are what you were taught and believe?

The Limit Is When You Say Stop™

Day Eight

Distance Judging

Judge not, that ye be not judged. Matthew 7:1

The appearance of an individual can sometimes surprise you about who they are. I am sure that many of us have met someone whom we thought was a certain type of person. For example, mean, kind, temperamental, cocky, etc... Sometimes, after getting to know the person, we find out that they are the total opposite. Many folks have been through many situations that cause them to act a certain way, which doesn't really define who they are. Getting to know someone for yourself and not relying on another person's experience with that individual, can sometimes cause you to think differenty.

The chemistry you may have with one individual may be different from someone else's. Of course, if a person is notorious for certain unwanted acts, you should avoid them. However, getting to know someone will put you on the path to making the right decisions, in the event of any possible future encounters with that individual. The consequence of distance judging can sometimes cause unnecessary hurt as well as disconnect you from some of the best people you will ever meet. Instead of judging someone, take time to get to know them.

Today's Focus

- ❖ The appearance of an individual can sometimes send the wrong message of who they are.
- ❖ Never judge a person based on appearance.
- ❖ One person's experience with an individual may not be the same as yours.
- ❖ Get to know someone before you judge them.

Reflection

❖ Do you judge people from a distance?
❖ Do you seek other people's opinion about someone before you befriend them?
❖ Have you ever met someone who seems to be one way and after getting to know them they were the total opposite?

Distance Judging

Reflection

- Do you judge people from a distance?
- Do you seek other people's opinions about someone before you befriend them?
- Have you ever met someone who seems to be one way and after getting to know them they were the total opposite?

The Limit Is When You Say Stop™

It's My Time

I will praise thee; for I am fearfully and wonderfully made: marvelous are thy works; and that my soul knoweth right well. Psalm 139:14

The rituals and responsibilities of life keeps us moving at a faster pace the longer we live and the more we accomplish. I once had a conversation with one of the most famous people that ever lived. While we were talking, I remember she summarized the difference between having problems when you are poor versus when you are rich. According to her, "When you are poor with problems, it takes a little money to fix them, but when you are rich with problems, you go broke trying to fix them." Therefore, rich or poor, problems will always be there. As the saying goes, new level, new devil.

Often times we spend so much time worrying about the world and others, we forget about ourselves. Too often people work 24/7 to have a particular lifestyle, but at the same time they have no quality life outside of work. Working tirelessly without taking time for rest, family and vacations is not a quality life. Take time to love and cherish yourself, because you only live once. No matter what your task, there will always be more to do. Your body is a temple of the Holy Spirit, so give yourself the best.

Today's Focus

- ❖ The pace of the world will only get faster, so try to find the time to relax and enjoy the beauty of God's creation (nature).
- ❖ No matter how much you get done, there will still be more to do.
- ❖ Your body is a temple of the Holy Spirit, so cherish and care for it.

Reflection

- Do you find yourself chasing after the newest technology?
- Do you put work before health?
- Do you find yourself worrying about others, while forgetting about yourself?
- Do you take time for family and friends?

Reflection

- ❖ Do you find yourself chasing after the newest technology?
- ❖ Do you put work before health?
- ❖ Do you find yourself worrying about others, while forgetting about yourself?
- ❖ Do you take time for family and friends?

The Limit Is When You Say Stop™

Day Ten

Our Relationship

Whether therefore ye eat, or drink, or whatsoever ye do, do all to the glory of God. 1 Corinthians 10:31

Hi, hope you are feeling ok when you read this. I know it's been a while since you actually thought about me, but I am still here waiting for you to give me some needed attention. There are a few things that I have been meaning to say to you, but you are always busy. Every time we go out to eat, we go to the same fast food restaurant. You know I need fruits, nuts and vegetables, but according to you, it's not necessary. We haven't had a good night rest in a long time. The last time we went shopping, you spent $250.00 on clothes and $3.00 on lunch. I ask you for water, you give me soda, beer and juice. I can't believe you are embarrassed to walk with me, maybe it's the reason we don't exercise anymore. I wish you would give me something organic instead of the chemically filled stuff you give to me. I understand it costs less, so I guess you would rather give the savings to the doctor. This morning you told me you weren't feeling well, but I hope it goes away on its own, since you don't believe in doctors. There is so much more I could say, but I have to stop now because I am losing energy. Oh! I know you probably don't remember my name so let me remind you, my last name is *BODY* and my first name is *YOUR*.

Today's Focus

- ❖ The attention one pays to their body will either make or break their health.
- ❖ The choice is yours to make sure you feed your body the proper foods. You should have plenty of Fruits, Nuts, and Vegetables, along with lots of rest, clean drinking water and exercise.
- ❖ The money you save by feeding your body junk food will be given to your doctor and it will be even more depending on the diagnosis.

Reflection

- ❖ Do you take the time to make sure your body is being taken care of?
- ❖ Do you read nutrition charts/ labels before purchasing packaged foods?
- ❖ Do you exercise at least 3 times a week?
- ❖ Do you take time to prepare healthy meals on a daily basis?

Reflection

- Do you take the time to make sure your body is being taken care of?
- Do you read nutrition charts/ labels before purchasing packaged foods?
- Do you exercise at least 3 times a week?
- Do you take time to prepare healthy meals on a daily basis?

Reflection

- Do you take the time to make sure your body is being taken care of?
- Do you read nutrition charts/ labels before purchasing packaged foods?
- Do you exercise at least 3 times a week?
- Do you take time to prepare healthy meals on a daily basis?

The Limit Is When You Say Stop™

Imaginary Wall

*I will not leave you ᵀcomfortless: I will come to you.
St. John 14:18*

As humans, from the moment we were born to the moment we realize our existence, we automatically develop an imaginary wall around us that will set the boundaries for the years to come. Depending on the environment, in which we were brought up, the size of that imaginary wall will differ. If one was brought up in a supportive, stable and loving environment, they will, in some cases, have fewer issues with future relationships and will tend to see life on a wider spectrum, because the love and support helped build self-confidence. On the other hand, there are individuals who were brought up in a non-loving and non-supportive environment, which may promote a narrow spectrum, and causes struggle in their relationships, because they are constantly trying to find the median between acceptance and rejection, success and failure. At some point, both individuals may encounter the task of dealing with each other, which may yield unpredictable results. However, the understanding and the acceptance of each other can help both individuals overcome their differences.

Too often, we fall victim thinking that we are the only one going through whatever circumstances we may be facing, which is never the case. If you are reading this, you are alive and you have your own struggles which you hope others will understand when you explain it to them.

Therefore, there are others around you who are experiencing similar situations. Having an open mind with understanding and listening twice as you speak, will help you to overcome the challenges of life.

Today's Focus

- ❖ Having an open mind will help us to understand that we are what we were taught and believe.
- ❖ It's ok to trust and love the people who exercise such actions towards us.
- ❖ You are not the only one going through life's struggles.

Reflection

- ❖ Do you avoid making friends with the people you meet?
- ❖ Do you struggle with the pains of yesterday?
- ❖ Are you constantly beating yourself up about not being good enough?

Reflection

❖ Do you avoid making friends with the people you meet?
❖ Do you struggle with the pains of yesterday?
❖ Are you constantly beating yourself up about not being good enough?

Reflection

- ❖ Do you avoid making friends with the people you meet?
- ❖ Do you struggle with the pains of yesterday?
- ❖ Are you constantly beating yourself up about not being good enough?

The Limit Is When You Say Stop™

Day Twelve

A Word

Let no corrupt communication proceed out of your mouth, but that which is good to the use of edifying, that it may minister grace unto the hearers. Ephesians 4:29

Words are like water it can either give life or take life. Many have quit projects, jobs, relationships, etc… because of a word that someone threw at them. It is very difficult to forget something that someone said, especially if it is the one thing you struggle with the most. One way of preventing certain trigger words from affecting you is by being vigilant of the people you choose to discuss your situations with. Most of the time we have no control over what comes surprisingly. There are hurting folks who like to see others hurt, and they will not hesitate to exercise their hurtful ways when the moment presents itself.

On the other hand, there are positive words which can cause a person to achieve heights they never thought possible. Almost everyone who has accomplished a goal, has heard that one voice in their head that filled them with such encouragement while they were toiling. Therefore, words can either kill or heal, so be mindful of the words you choose when conversing with others. *Be known for your greatness!*

Today's Focus

- ❖ Words can heal or kill so choose your words carefully.
- ❖ Don't discuss personal issues with folks you don't know.
- ❖ You are wonderfully made by God so don't give listening ears to bad words one may throw at you.
- ❖ Be known for your greatness.

Reflection

- Are you mindful of the words you choose when you are angry?
- Have you ever had someone use a word at you that even to this day it still hurts you?
- Have you ever used a word at someone that you wish you could take back?
- How does it feel to be called a bad word?

Reflection

- Are you mindful of the words you choose when you are angry?
- Have you ever had someone use a word at you that even to this day it still hurts you?
- Have you ever used a word at someone that you wish you could take back?
- How does it feel to be called a bad word?

The Limit Is When You Say Stop™

Self-Image

26: And God said, let us make man in our image, after our likeness: And let them have dominion over the fish of the sea, and over the fowl of the air, and over the cattle, and over all the earth, and over every creeping thing that creepeth upon the earth. 27: So God created man in his own image, in the image of God created he him; male and female created he them. Genesis 1:26-27

Have you ever found yourself in a situation where everything is just going according to plan and suddenly that one thing just comes out of no where and brings everything to a halt? This can sometimes be very stressful, especially when you have put your all into it thus far. The ability to continue can sometimes be very discouraging, but you have to continue on your journey. As a result, the image that you have of yourself will now come into play. However you perceive yourself to be, will be the result that either makes or breaks the situation. You can't give birth to what you never conceived, therefore, whatever label you put on yourself that is what you will become. If you tell yourself you can't do it, you will only see the impossibility, but if you tell yourself you can do it, you will see the possibility. Never let the negative dwell in your mind, always think positive and keep a mental picture of what you want to achieve. Like in the story of creation, before God created man, He had an image of what He wanted man to look like. Therefore, if God can have an image of His future creation, who are we not to have an image of what we want our lives to be? When you change your negative self image, you will start seeing yourself as successful, strong and happy.

Today's Focus

- ❖ Most people quit moments from success.
- ❖ Keeping a mental picture of what you want to accomplish will help to keep you focused and determined.
- ❖ Nothing good comes easy. It takes hard work, persistence and faith to accomplish your goals.
- ❖ The journey maybe long but the success is sweeter than honey.

Reflection

- ❖ How do you deal with setbacks?
- ❖ Do you have a mental image of what you are trying to accomplish?
- ❖ Do you believe in yourself?

Reflection

❖ How do you deal with setbacks?
❖ Do you have a mental image of what you are trying to accomplish?
❖ Do you believe in yourself?

Self-Image

Reflection

- ❖ How do you deal with setbacks?
- ❖ Do you have a mental image of what you are trying to accomplish?
- ❖ Do you believe in yourself?

The Limit Is When You Say Stop™

Day Fourteen

Emotional Bondage

Commit thy way unto the Lord; trust also in him; and he shall bring it to pass. Psalm 37:5

Every person alive has two sides to their memory bank, good memories and bad memories. Knowing how to manage your memory bank is extremely important. The choice to be happy or sad will be determined by the memory bank you decide to withdraw from. One of the worse practices is self-pity because it can rob you of your future and joy. Too often, we meet people who are stuck in a phase of their life and all they do is dwell on it so much that it prevents them from moving forward. Don't get me wrong, it's ok to share with someone your life experiences, but when someone uses a bad experience to hold their life hostage, they are only wasting their precious days given to them by God. Things that could have been, relationships that would have been, are what they are. There are unexplained reasons why certain things happen such as losing a loved one, a pet, a job, a broken marriage, or even a body part. Sometimes we can't find the answers, but if we pick up the broken pieces and continue to move forward we will eventually get the answers we yearned for.

Some people were brought up in homes where they were abused mentally, physically, sexually and emotionally. There are no excuses for such conditions.

If you are one of these individuals, please understand you are not your past and letting go, as hard as it may be, will bring you into a new world of great potential and joy. When you are hurting, it sometimes takes over your existence so much, that it shows in every aspect of your life, which sometimes may work against you by having people avoid you. This may then limit your opportunities. Withdrawing from the good memories will allow you to shine and move forward in a positive light, attracting more people to you. No matter how hard things may be, keeping a positive attitude will help you to tap into your true potential. Every champion, after finishing a competition, always emphasizes how surprised they were about what they have accomplished and that's because they have allowed themselves to be free. As we all know, if you free your mind, everything will fall into place

Today's Focus

- ❖ The memory bank that you choose to withdraw from will decide how you process your thoughts.
- ❖ The choice to be happy or sad lies in your thought life.
- ❖ Let go of the past so you can embrace your future.
- ❖ When you stay stuck on what could have been, you are only wasting time. Accept it and move on because there are brighter days ahead.

Reflection

- How do you manage your memory bank?
- Do you want to be happy or sad?
- Are you stuck on something that could have been?
- Are you crowding your mind with negative thoughts?

Reflection

- How do you manage your memory bank?
- Do you want to be happy or sad?
- Are you stuck on something that could have been?
- Are you crowding your mind with negative thoughts?

Reflection

- ❖ How do you manage your memory bank?
- ❖ Do you want to be happy or sad?
- ❖ Are you stuck on something that could have been?
- ❖ Are you crowding your mind with negative thoughts?

The Limit Is When You Say Stop™

Too Good to be True

Many are the afflictions of the righteous: but the Lord delivereth him out of them all. Psalm 34:19

One day, I was having a conversation with a friend of mine. While conversing and reflecting on our college years together, he was constantly talking about how difficult his life was. He also kept talking about how poor he was while in college. Being the positive-minded one in the discussion, I asked him, "Why do you always talk about how poor you were in college?"

He replied, "Because I can't get it out of my mind."

I then asked him, "Why is this always on your mind, considering all that you have been through?" That's when he told me that his mother never helped him and she always discouraged him by telling him that he will never be anything in this world. Therefore, every time he suffers a set back he can only hear his mother's voice telling him he will never be anything in this world. I then asked him, "Why did you finish college?"

He said, "Because I wanted to better my life." So I asked him, "How would you describe your current life style?"

He replied, "I am not in need of anything." I then explained to him that he was not celebrating the good times or his accomplishments, instead, he was refusing to embrace his blessings. Also, I mentioned to him that if he continued to dwell on his past he would not enjoy the present or the future. That's when the lights went on and he said, "WOW! You are right, why didn't I think of that?"

When your life is going great, don't ask why, *enjoy the moment because tomorrow you may die.*

There are so many people who dwell on one phase/occurrence of their life, that no matter how accomplished they are, they can never see it, because they are stuck in past times. It's time to get up and move on. Keep your past in the past and embrace your success by celebrating every waking moment. Living in the past will only rob you of the good moments that await you. Take time to celebrate yourself and always remember, LOVE is like a million dollars, if you don't have it for yourself you can't give it.

Today's Focus

- ❖ Always find time to celebrate the good times with family and friends.
- ❖ The past made you who you are today, so be thankful for the experiences you gain because now you can make wise choices.
- ❖ Dwelling on the past will cause you to ignore the blessings of the present.
- ❖ Love is like a million bucks, if you don't have it for yourself you can't give it.

Reflection

- ❖ Do you celebrate the good times with friends and family?
- ❖ Are you thankful for past experiences?
- ❖ Do you dwell on the past?
- ❖ Do you have love for yourself?

Reflection

- ❖ Do you celebrate the good times with friends and family?
- ❖ Are you thankful for past experiences?
- ❖ Do you dwell on the past?
- ❖ Do you have love for yourself?

Reflection

- ❖ Do you celebrate the good times with friends and family?
- ❖ Are you thankful for past experiences?
- ❖ Do you dwell on the past?
- ❖ Do you have love for yourself?

The Limit Is When You Say Stop™

Day Sixteen

Angels in the Dark

A new commandment I give unto you, That ye love one another; as I have loved you, that ye also love one another.
St. John 13:34

The story was told of a man who lived in America and got arrested, for a minor traffic violation. While in jail, he was forced to share a cell with a group of men from Africa. The Africans never spoke much English so communication was at a minimum. Out of curiosity, one of the men from Africa asked the American, "What are you in for sir?"

The American replied, "Some traffic stuff." The American then asked the African the same question. The African then replied, "We are all from Africa and we were selling street goods without a permit so the cops caught us and brought us here." Suddenly, the warden knocked on the door of the jail and asked if anyone would like to order dinner. The American said he was ok. One of the African men then asked the warden, "What kind of food can we order?" The warden replied, "Chinese." The African said, "Ok, let me get the menu."

After a few minutes of deliberation, the Africans placed their orders. When the food came, one of the African said to the American, "My brother, you need to eat with us please!"

The American said, "I don't eat Chinese food." Then the African replied, "Come on brother we can't eat without you, because back home in our tribe we don't eat until everyone around us is served." The American still refused. Then the African started doing the unthinkable, he began to separate some food in an empty container for the American, just in case he got hungry as the night went on.

Once the African men graced their food, one of the Africans said to the American, "Brother you are far away from home but I will pray for your return." Meaning the American has to get back to loving and sharing with his fellowman. The American was speechless because he was not use to such kindness.

People find themselves in situations at times that they never even thought they would ever be in, even though it may seem as if it's the worse day of their life, there is always a lesson to be learned.

Sometimes God puts us through situations so as to help us to see the message He's been trying to relay to us. So with this in mind, one of the worse things to do is to judge a person based on the situation they are in without getting the full story. No matter what the situation may be, you will always have your gaurdian angel beside you, just like the American. So stop! Be calm and listen to the little voices that are trying to get your attention. Always remember, the hardest thing to do is the right thing and the easiest thing to do is the wrong thing.

Today's Focus

- ❖ The worst of situations can be one of the best life lessons.
- ❖ Be kind to the people you meet because you may be entertaining angels.
- ❖ Never judge a person without first getting to know them.
- ❖ A kind act can change a person's outlook on life for the better.

Reflection

- ❖ Are you quick to give up when faced with hard times?
- ❖ How do you treat strangers?
- ❖ Do you like to judge others?
- ❖ Do you find joy in being kind to your fellowman?

Reflection

❖ Are you quick to give up when faced with hard times?
❖ How do you treat strangers?
❖ Do you like to judge others?
❖ Do you find joy in being kind to your fellowman?

Reflection

- ❖ Are you quick to give up when faced with hard times?
- ❖ How do you treat strangers?
- ❖ Do you like to judge others?
- ❖ Do you find joy in being kind to your fellowman?

The Limit Is When You Say Stop™

Day Seventeen

Two of a Kind

Have mercy upon me, O God, according to thy lovingkindess: according unto the multitude of thy tender mercies blot out my transgressions. Psalm 51:1

One Saturday morning, I was running late for church. While on the highway I was thinking, "What excuses am I going to give my pastor for not being on time," considering he had asked me to assist with the collecting of the day's tithes and offerings. As I approached my exit, I encountered a massive traffic back up leading to the off ramp that I needed to take. From a distance, I could see an opening all the way in front of the line of traffic which would involve me cutting in front of everyone in order to get into that opening. There was enough space to commit the act, but my conscience kept telling me no. Then low and behold, about four cars blew by me and did exactly what I was thinking of doing. "That's it, 'game's on!," I thought to myself. So I pulled out the line of traffic and headed toward the front of the line. I saw the perfect opening, so I went for it. As I was about to complete my move, the guy driving the vehicle I wanted to get in front of, saw me coming and accelerated in hopes of preventing me from getting in front of him. I knew my car was much more powerful than his, so I wasn't concerned about him preventing me from getting in front of his vehicle, which I did with ease. Obviously, he was not pleased that I got in front of him. After exiting, he tried cutting me off several times. I said to myself, "Bring it on!" So after going at it for a while, cutting each other off, we both calm down.

A few miles later, I noticed he was still driving behind me. Finally, I came to the turn that lead into my church's parking lot. As I stopped to turn into the parking lot, I realized he was doing the same.
I then pulled into the lot and positioned my car in a parking space, with my eyes fixed in my rear view mirror watching his every move, I couldn't help but to notice him pulling into a parking space also and positioning his vehicle as if he had reached his destination. I started asking myself, "Who could that be?" Then it dawned on me, he was a visitor visiting my church! I was so embarrassed of my actions, that I sat in my car hoping he would go inside the church before I did, but instead, he also sat in his car. I then decided that I am going to just walk as fast as I can so as not to even look at him. As soon as I was nearing his car he got out and started heading towards the church. I was speechless and so was he. Out of embarrassment, we kept looking straight and never exchanged a word; not even a good morning. Later on that day, while I was collecting the day's tithes and offerings, I felt even worse when I got to his pew with the offering plate. I couldn't look at him and he couldn't look at me. To this day we never confronted each other and I never saw him again.

Be careful of how you treat the ones around you because they may share in your weakness and even though we may know better, it's sometimes hard to resist saying or doing something out of line. We are all people living in a world with trials that sometimes causes us to go off track. So in the future, keep in mind the influence your actions may encourage.

Today's Focus

- Sometimes the littlest thing we do, that seems to be harmless, though we know deep down is wrong, may create the biggest problems in life.
- Patience is a virtue.
- Do unto others as you would have them do to you.
- It's a small world. The people you hurt today may be the ones you need tomorrow.

Reflection

- ❖ Do you always think before you act?
- ❖ Are you a patient person?
- ❖ Do you practice doing good for your fellowman?
- ❖ Do you agree that the people you hurt today may be the ones you need tomorrow?

Reflection

- Do you always think before you act?
- Are you a patient person?
- Do you practice doing good for your fellowman?
- Do you agree that the people you hurt today may be the ones you need tomorrow?

The Limit Is When You Say Stop™

Day Eighteen

Our Independence

Preserve me, O God: for in thee do I put my trust.
Psalm 16:1

Being independent doesn't mean that we can survive in the world on our own without the help from our fellowman. The real meaning of independence is being in control and making preparations for your needs and having a system to sustain you, such as a job or business. Even though you may have a job or business, you still need the assistance of others to execute. Standing on your own does come with challenges, such as sacrificing your pleasure, in order to reach the goal of being independent. So staying focused and determined with a generous amount of "PLEASE" and "THANK YOU," will greatly pay off. Always remember, "Anyone who considers themselves independent of everyone is a fool destined towards loneliness and failure."

Today's Focus

- ❖ No matter who you are and what you are trying to accomplish, you will need the assistance of others.
- ❖ Always show appreciation to the people who have helped and are helping you to grow.
- ❖ A kind word can move mountains.
- ❖ Always remember to say "PLEASE" and "THANKS."

Reflection

- ❖ Have you ever asked for help?
- ❖ Do you show appreciation to the people who are there for you?
- ❖ Do you make it your practice to say, "PLEASE" and "THANKS?"

Our Independence

Reflection

❖ Have you ever asked for help?
❖ Do you show appreciation to the people who are there for you?
❖ Do you make it your practice to say, "PLEASE" and "THANKS?"

The Limit Is When You Say Stop™

What about Me?

5: But I have trusted in thy mercy; my heart shall rejoice in thy salvation. 6: I will sing unto the Lord, because he hath dealt bountifully with me. Psalm 13:5-6

Almost everyone in the world looks forward to celebrating Christmas. Beyond the fine foods, meeting and greeting family and friends, there is that little question that dangles in our minds, "What gifts am I getting this year?" To partially satisfy our curiosity, we look at the name(s) on the gift(s) lying under the tree. Strangely, the larger gift(s) normally grab our attention at first. In the end, it doesn't matter which gift(s) you like based on its appearance. The fact is, you can only have the gift(s) with your name on it.

Often times, we encounter people around us who sometimes have the things we desire the most, which sometimes may cause us to devalue or ignore our blessings given to us by God. Like the gifts of Christmas, God will place your name on your blessing. So be anxious for nothing. Keep your goals in sight knowing that all good things come from God and with hard work and determination you will accomplish whatever you set out to do. Never let another person's accomplishments cause you to look down on yourself. We are all on a different journey, which makes us unique and special in many different ways. Always give thanks for what you have because no matter how little it may seem, there are others out there who wish they could have what you got.

Today's Focus

- ❖ God will never keep a good thing from you.
- ❖ Your sustenance comes from God, not man.
- ❖ Never let what people have, cause you to devalue or ignore what God has provided for you.
- ❖ With persistence and faith, *The Limit is When You Say Stop.*™

Reflection

- ❖ Do you have faith in God?
- ❖ Do you agree that whatever you 'need' God will provide?
- ❖ Do you believe in yourself?

Reflection

❖ Do you have faith in God?
❖ Do you agree that whatever you 'need' God will provide?
❖ Do you believe in yourself?

Reflection

- Do you have faith in God?
- Do you agree that whatever you 'need' God will provide?
- Do you believe in yourself?

The Limit Is When You Say Stop™

Your Efforts

Be ye strong therefore, and let not your hands be weak: for your work shall be rewarded. 2 Chronicles 15:7

Your accomplishments will be reflected by your effort. The task of doing something can sometimes yield unpredictable results, therefore, preparing for the worst case scenerio can sometimes prevent us from becoming discouraged. Nothing in life that's worth keeping comes easy, so one has to apply more effort the closer they get to their goals. The feeling of discouragement is natural when faced with difficulties, but, in most cases, if one should just take a moment to reflect on where they are coming from, they will soon realize that they have come too far to turn back now. The point is, try not to focus on where you are, instead, focus on where you are going.

Surrounding yourself with like-minded individuals and constantly seeking new information, can yield great benefits such as ideas and strategies. When all is said and done, it's better to try and fail, than fail to try. The largest brick building was not made with one big brick, rather, it was created brick by brick. So every step you take towards attaining your goal, is similar to the laying of those bricks. With a positive attitude and faith, opportunities are endless. So keep pressing on, because your day of victory awaits you.

Today's Focus

- ❖ Whatever efforts applied, will be measured by your accomplishments.
- ❖ Prepare for the worst and hope for the best, in doing so, you won't be as disappointed if things don't go according to plan.
- ❖ The closer you get to your goal, the harder things will get.
- ❖ Surround yourself with people who are in your field. This will help you when you need information and support.

Reflection

- ❖ Are you applying enough effort towards your goal?
- ❖ Do you have a Plan B in case things don't work out?
- ❖ Do you set time limits on achieving your goal?
- ❖ Are you surrounding yourself with like-minded individuals?

Your Efforts

Reflection

❖ Are you applying enough effort towards your goal?
❖ Do you have a Plan B in case things don't work out?
❖ Do you set time limits on achieving your goal?
❖ Are you surrounding yourself with like-minded individuals?

Reflection

❖ Are you applying enough effort towards your goal?
❖ Do you have a Plan B in case things don't work out?
❖ Do you set time limits on achieving your goal?
❖ Are you surrounding yourself with like-minded individuals?

Your Efforts

The Limit Is When You Say Stop™

Day Twenty-One

The Ladder of Life!

For the arms of the wicked shall be broken: but the Lord upholdeth the righteous. Psalm 37:17

There are two types of people who climb the ladder of life. One who climbs with a hammer and knocks off each rung the higher they go, not leaving a way for people to follow behind. This is a person who never helps or shows appreciation and/or gratitude to anyone, not even the folks who have either helped or are still helping them in attaining their dreams/goals. On the other hand, there is one who climbs the ladder of life with a rope and extends a hand to the ones behind. This is a person who is always quick to help someone in need, while showing gratitude and appreciation to the folks who have either helped or are helping them to attain their dreams/goals. If hard times should occur, the person with the hammer will fall harder with no help and support on their way down, while the person with the rope will always have someone to call on in the time of need. Take an honest look at your life, now decide which of the these two people best describes who you are. Remember, the people you meet on your way up, you will meet on your way down.

Today's Focus

- ❖ The people who are there for you should be treated with respect and be recognized for their efforts.
- ❖ Be quick to help and always offer an encouraging word to your fellowman.
- ❖ The people you meet on your way up, you will meet on your way down; so be mindful of how you treat the ones around you.

Reflection

- Do you practice showing respect to the people around you?
- Are you quick to help and offer support?
- Do you believe that with success there is also the possibility for failure?

Reflection

- Do you practice showing respect to the people around you?
- Are you quick to help and offer support?
- Do you believe that with success there is also the possibility for failure?

The Limit Is When You Say Stop™

Day Twenty-Two

Heart of a Champion

Have not I commanded thee? Be strong and of a good courage; be not afraid, neither be thou dismayed: for the LORD thy God is with thee whithersoever thou goest.
Joshua 1:9

Conditioning of the mind, is one of the most valuable assets for a champion. The connection of the heart and mind will be seen in the performance of the body. The ability to stay focused, disciplined, alert and conscious will also determine the results of a champion's capability. In a champion's mind, there is no room for failure, only winning. Even though struggles may arrive, it will soon be overridden by a higher level of training and preparedness. When defeat enters the equation, a real champion will rise and review his/her mistakes/weaknesses and correct it. This strengthens him/her to get ready for the next challenge. Staying defeated will only rob you of what you have built thus far. The choice is yours to rise to the occasion and face your demons or fall in failure. The hurt will be bitter but victory is always sweet.

Today's Focus

- ❖ Conditioning of the mind is the key to success.
- ❖ The connection between heart and mind will be seen in your actions.
- ❖ When failure enters your mind, it should be erased with positive thinking. Staying defeated will rob you of what you have built thus far.
- ❖ You will be defined by your legacy.

Reflection

- Do you condition your mind to think success and not failure?
- Do you dwell on the negative or the positive?
- What legacy are you creating?
- What legacy are you leaving behind?

Reflection

- Do you condition your mind to think success and not failure?
- Do you dwell on the negative or the positive?
- What legacy are you creating?
- What legacy are you leaving behind?

The Limit Is When You Say Stop™

Day Twenty-Three

Thank You

It is a good thing to give thanks unto the Lord, and to sing praises unto thy name, O most High. Psalm 92:1

It is the simplest way to show someone how much they are appreciated. Yet, there are so many people who seldomly say, "Thank You," when their needs are met. Amongst the basic principles taught in the early years of a child's life "Thank you" is one of the most familiar.

Things get even more interesting when the same individuals keep going back to the same sources for help, with the same bad practice of not saying, "Thank you." Being self-centered and selfish are two of the main causes for someone to display such actions. Eventually, they will notice that they are receiving more "No" than "Yes," because more and more people have realized their ungrateful ways.

A simple "Thank You" can make your life experiences very pleasant, because most people will want to help you when you are known to be a generous and appreciative individual. The negativity of this world will work in your favor when you say, "Thank you," because it makes you stand out from amongst the folks who seldomly say, "Thank you," and for that reason you will always be remembered in a positive way. Everyone likes to feel appreciated, so always remember to say, "Thank you."

Remember, the man who threw the stone always forgets where it lands but the man who got hit, will always remember the location and hurt. Your "Thank you" today will be remembered tomorrow.

Today's Focus

- ❖ Saying, "Thank you" is the simplest way to show your appreciation.
- ❖ Individuals who do not practice saying, "Thank you" will eventually realize that they are getting more "No" than "Yes."
- ❖ A simple "Thank You" can make one's life experiences very pleasant.
- ❖ Your "Thank You" today will not be forgotten tomorrow.

Reflection

- Do you practice saying, "Thank you?"
- How does it feel when you do someone a favor and they don't say, "Thank you?"

Reflection

- Do you practice saying, "Thank you?"
- How does it feel when you do someone a favor and they don't say, "Thank you?"

Thank You

Reflection

- Do you practice saying, "Thank you?"
- How does it feel when you do someone a favor and they don't say, "Thank you?"

The Limit Is When You Say Stop™

Day Twenty-Four

Success Pill

Humble yourselves in the sight of the Lord, and He shall lift you up. James 4:10

We live in a world where there are pills for almost everything. For example weight loss, memory loss, adult personal enhancement, sleeping and the list goes on. To this date, I have never heard or seen a pill for success. Therefore, to be what you want to be in this world, you have to stay focused and work diligently towards attaining such heights. Success starts in the mind. Remember, that just because you can't see something happening, doesn't mean that it is impossible. A vision is critical for your dreams to come true. If your insecurities and fears will not allow you to see past your dreams, it will not seem attainable. Instead, focus on something that you are passionate about. When God made man, He made man in his own image, therefore, He had a mental image of what He wanted man to look like. When He was satisfied with His plan He then put it into action. As there are side effects in taking pills, not being proactive and focused will produce stagnation which leads to you becoming less than your true potential. Take action and be your success pill.

Today's Focus

- ❖ Of all the pills we have in society, there are no pills for success. Always work diligently towards your success.
- ❖ Success starts in the mind.
- ❖ Just because you can't see yourself doing something, doesn't mean it is impossible, a vision is critical for your dreams to come true.
- ❖ Always have an image of what you are trying to accomplish.

Reflection

- Do you believe that success starts in the mind?
- Do you have a mental image of what it is that you want to accomplish?
- Do you believe you can do it?

Reflection

- ❖ Do you believe that success starts in the mind?
- ❖ Do you have a mental image of what it is that you want to accomplish?
- ❖ Do you believe you can do it?

The Limit Is When You Say Stop™

Day Twenty-Five

Greed and Pride

Blessed is the man that endureth temptation: for when he is tried, he shall receive the crown of life, which the Lord hath promised to them that love him. James 1:12

Every conflict known to man is a factor of greed and/or pride. We live in a world where **bigger**, *newer*, *prettier*, **bolder**, etc... are considered to be better. So, many folks abandon valuable things such as cars, clothes, homes, etc... for the next hot item. Some even abandon their families in the quest for more. After acquiring such items, they soon realize that there is a newer version soon to be available, which puts them back on the never ending **greed trail**. When pride is introduced, the situation gets even worse because they now have to maintain the title of being the person with the newer, bigger, most expensive items, which may put unnecessary pressure on them by making them constantly worry about what the world thinks of them.

Life is meant to be enjoyed, not rushed. Material things will never make you happy, instead, it will only give you a moment of temporary satisfaction. You were born into this world empty-handed thus you will die empty-handed. Therefore, whatever you obtain in this world, you cannot take with you when you die. Be satisfied, value what you have and give thanks to God for He is our provider; this will bring you inner peace and joy.

Today's Focus

- ❖ Every conflict stems from greed and/or pride.
- ❖ The hottest items that you can think of right now will eventually give way to something much more hot and happening.
- ❖ Never abandon your family for material gains.
- ❖ Having the biggest and best items, will not bring you happiness it will only offer you a moment of temporary of satisfaction.
- ❖ Learn to appreciate what you have.

Reflection

- Are you constantly trying to obtain the hottest items available so as to maintain your identity?
- Do you take time aside to spend with your family?
- Do you only feel happy and appreciated when you are the one with the most abundance while amongst your peers?
- Do you appreciate what you have?

Reflection

- Are you constantly trying to obtain the hottest items available so as to maintain your identity?
- Do you take time aside to spend with your family?
- Do you only feel happy and appreciated when you are the one with the most abundance while amongst your peers?
- Do you appreciate what you have?

Reflection

- Are you constantly trying to obtain the hottest items available so as to maintain your identity?
- Do you take time aside to spend with your family?
- Do you only feel happy and appreciated when you are the one with the most abundance while amongst your peers?
- Do you appreciate what you have?

The Limit Is When You Say Stop™

Day Twenty-Six

Quitting

I can do all things through Christ which strengtheneth me.
Philippians 4:13

One of the easiest ways to quit is by deciding to take a break. In some cases, it's the feeling of 'it's taking too long' or 'it will never happen.' This is the point when you lose your desire to continue because of some form of discouragement, so using the excuse 'I am taking a break' seems valid for the moment. While some folks may have the ability to get back to completing what they started, most will not. The road to success is not easy, so be prepared, patient and stay focused. Never compare yourself to anyone because your journey may be different. Every successful person has a story to tell and no two are alike. Even though there may be common points, there are still differences. Think of all the people you know who are successful, now ask yourself, "What if they had quit moments before their break through?" Well, that's what happens to many folks. Surround yourself with positive people and be prepared to take advantage of the slightest opportunities that come your way.

Today's Focus

- Be careful when deciding to take a break. Sometimes this can lead to stagnation which may cause you to discontinue your project.
- The road to success is not easy. You have to be prepared and patient while staying focused.
- Never compare yourself to anyone because your journey will never be like any other, it will be an individual experience and a learning process.
- Many people quit moments before their break through.
- **Don't quit.**

Reflection

- Have you taken a break from something you wanted to accomplish and you still find yourself saying you need to get back doing what you were doing?
- Do you find yourself focused on others and their success? *You must stop!*
- Are you thinking of quitting a current project because you feel like it will never happen?

Reflection

❖ Have you taken a break from something you wanted to accomplish and you still find yourself saying you need to get back doing what you were doing?

❖ Do you find yourself focused on others and their success? *You must stop!*

❖ Are you thinking of quitting a current project because you feel like it will never happen?

The Limit Is When You Say Stop™

Day Twenty-Seven

Hidden Talents

Neglect not the gift that is in thee, which was given thee by prophecy, with the laying on of the hands of the presbytery. 1 Timothy 4:14

Have you ever done something and have people talking about it over and over? Does it leave you asking yourself questions, like, "What is the big deal?" Or "Are they just trying to make me feel good?" Your natural talent will bring you a relaxed feeling when being executed. It is so much fun that, even if you are working, it doesn't feel like work, instead, it's the feeling of enjoyment.

Sometimes we spend time doing things that don't bring out our natural talent. As humans, we automatically gravitate to the things we feel best defines us. However, we may still miss our calling because we are doing what we do for reasons other than passion. The things we excel at normally come from a passion deep within us. Sometimes I get asked the same question over and over by many people, "How do I know what my talent is, because I am good at a lot of different things?" My answer has been and always will be, "Whatever you love to do and do not think of getting paid for it, because your satisfaction comes from just doing it, that is your talent." Now the real joy comes from when you take that talent and turn it into an income. Unfortunately, there are cases where individuals have to take whatever job is available.

Still, taking time to develop your natural talent will yield more satisfaction rather than compromise. We all have our own talent but if left undeveloped, it will go to the richest place on earth, the *cemetery*. If all neglected talents and ideas, that lie in graves, could be currency, this world would be abundant in wealth. So always take time to develop your talent.

Today's Focus

- Your natural talent is what you enjoy doing with passion, even if it's for free.
- Try not to spend too much time on things that don't bring out your natural talent.
- The richest place on earth is the *cemetery* because of all the undeveloped talents. Take time today to develop your talent.

Reflection

- ❖ What is the one thing you would do for free all day and be fulfilled?
- ❖ Are you spending time and energy on something that you really don't care about?
- ❖ Do you know your talent?
- ❖ Are you spending time developing your talent?

Reflection

- What is the one thing you would do for free all day and be fulfilled?
- Are you spending time and energy on something that you really don't care about?
- Do you know your talent?
- Are you spending time developing your talent?

Reflection

- What is the one thing you would do for free all day and be fulfilled?
- Are you spending time and energy on something that you really don't care about?
- Do you know your talent?
- Are you spending time developing your talent?

The Limit Is When You Say Stop™

Day Twenty-Eight

Aging Gracefully

19: What? No he not that your body is a temple of the Ho'ly Ghost which is in you, which ye have of God, and ye are not your own? 20: For ye are bought with a price: therefore glorify God in your body, and in your spirit, which are God's. 1 Corinthians 6:19-20

As the days go by, we look in the mirror and we sometimes notice the changes in our appearances. Depending on how we view life, our thoughts will vary. The process of aging can be controlled but not avoided. Therefore, we should give ourselves the best by making sure we get enough rest, excersise, drinking water and healthy foods, while limiting our stress levels.

Instead of feeling down about getting older, give God thanks that you are alive to see another day. I often times hear people ask God for guidance and protection and then, in another breath, complain about getting old, which I find to be very contradicting. No matter how old you are, there is a day coming when you will wish you could go back to being the age you are today and looking the way you do right now. Don't believe me? Okay, go ask your mama!

Today's Focus

- ❖ Once you are alive, you will get older.
- ❖ Aging can be controlled but not avoided.
- ❖ Make sure your body receives the best and healthiest foods, drinking water, excersise and lots of rest.
- ❖ Control your stress level.
- ❖ Be grateful you are still alive.
- ❖ One day you are going to wish you could look the way you do right now.

Reflection

- Are you constantly worrying about getting older?
- Do you make it your duty to take care of your body and health?
- Are you grateful to be alive?

Reflection

- ❖ Are you constantly worrying about getting older?
- ❖ Do you make it your duty to take care of your body and health?
- ❖ Are you grateful to be alive?

The Limit Is When You Say Stop™

Day Twenty-Nine

One Moment

5: Walk in wisdom toward them that are without, redeeming the time. 6: Let your speech be alway with grace, seasoned with salt, that ye may know how ye ought to answer every man. Colossians 4:5-6

We all have visions and dreams of how we want our lives to be, therefore, we apply ourselves accordingly. Often times, we meet people who have the same dreams and aspirations. Even the folks we've known from the past can sometimes cause us to say, "Really?" After finding out they are on the same path as we are, we sometimes are lead by visions and gathered information.

In the end, it all boils down to that One Moment in time when true worth will be put to the test. Learning to recognize the moment is the key to never taking a moment or anyone for granted. Sometimes the little moments and the people we least expected can be the combination that will lead us to our goal. Remember, read the message and not the messenger.

Today's Focus

- ❖ Start each day new with a clear mind and focus on how you can be a blessing to others, hence, you will be blessed.
- ❖ By being open-minded, positive and reaching out to people, you may find that One Moment will yield blessings not only for you but the other person as well.
- ❖ We all have visions and dreams of what we want to accomplish in life.
- ❖ There are others around you who may be on the same path who can assist you with your inquiries.
- ❖ Learning to recognize an opportunity is one of the key steps in obtaining your goals.
- ❖ Never take anyone or a good opportunity for granted.
- ❖ Remember the messenger has a message.

Reflection

- ❖ Do you have principles you live by?
- ❖ Do you have a vision of what you want to accomplish in life?
- ❖ Are you utilizing the resources around you in order to obtain the answers to your questions?
- ❖ Are you making use of the opportunities around you?
- ❖ Do you pay more attention to the messenger or the message?

Reflection

- Do you have principles you live by?
- Do you have a vision of what you want to accomplish in life?
- Are you utilizing the resources around you in order to obtain the answers to your questions?
- Are you making use of the opportunities around you?
- Do you pay more attention to the messenger or the message?

The Limit Is When You Say Stop™

Day Thirty

Student to Teacher

7: In all things shewing thyself a pattern of good works: in doctrine shewing uncorruptness, gravity, sincerity, 8: sound speech, that cannot be condemened; that he that is of the contrary part may be ashamed, having no evil thing to say of you. Titus 2:7-8

In the beginning stages, when a person is learning activities such as riding a bike, driving a car, swimming, etc… it is expected by the individual learning the task to be treated some what gentle. The instructor should understand that the individual is learning this for the first time, which is a common way to think. Strangely though, in some cases, students who were once taught without gentleness become instructors who are quick to throw the thought of being gentle out of the window when it is their time to teach. As a result, they often treat their students as if they should have known whatever they are trying to learn. Some instructors may even go as far as name calling, which is wrong and totally unnecessary. Everyone learns at a different pace, so patience is the fruit that an instructor needs before taking on such a task. The ability to get to know a student and their reason for wanting to learn a task may help in creating a strategy to accommodate their learning capacity, because what works for one student may not work for another. Remember, a soft answer can change a nation but harsh words start wars.

Today's Focus

- ❖ Everyone learns at a different pace, so patience is needed when people are being instructed.
- ❖ Name calling should never be a part of instructing someone.
- ❖ Never compare someone you are instructing to anyone else.
- ❖ Be patient today.

Reflection

- Do you exercise patience when teaching someone?
- Do you name call when someone doesn't understand?
- Do you compare someone you are instructing to others?
- Do you spend time getting to know the people you are instructing?

Reflection

❖ Do you exercise patience when teaching someone?
❖ Do you name call when someone doesn't understand?
❖ Do you compare someone you are instructing to others?
❖ Do you spend time getting to know the people you are instructing?

The Limit Is When You Say Stop™

Day Thirty-One

A Dying Wish

The Lord recompense thy work, and a full reward be given thee of the Lord God of Is'ra-el, under whose wings thou art come to trust. Ruth 2:12

One of the greatest experiences I ever had in my life was to speak to a very good neighbor and friend who was 73 years old and moments away from dying. I was home when his wife called me and she said, "He would like to speak with you before he dies." At first, I was very nervous and scared, I had all kinds of thoughts going through my mind about what our conversation was going to be like. As I entered the driveway, I got weaker every step I made on my way to his front door. Finally, I entered the house, then up the stairs and down the hallway. At this point, I am right outside the door leading to his bed room. The door was ajar, so I gently pushed it open, only to see a man who once looked so strong and vibrant weeks ago, to now see him lying in his bed dying. His features were alarming, he looked pale and weak. I didn't know if I should sit or stand because one part of me wanted to hurry and get out and the other part of me wanted to hear what he had to say.

He suddenly said to me, "Hey Malcolm, how are you?"

I said, "I am fine... and you?"

To my surprise he responded, "I am dying."

I said, "No you are not, you will be better soon."

Then he said, "Tomorrow this time I will be long gone, but I just wanted to say thanks for being such a good neighbor and friend. I always looked up to you as a hard worker and a honest man."

Tears came to my eyes as he continued.

Suddenly he bellowed out,

"God hates me, that's why He did this to me."

I said, "Did what?"

He said, "He gave me cancer."

I then asked him, "How old are you?"

He said, "73."

As I looked around the room, I saw people enter the room. I then asked, "And who are these people?"

He said, "They are my family."

I couldn't help but notice the brand new SUV parked in the driveway, along with such a beautiful house. I then asked him, "Who does it all belong to?"

He said, "Me."

I then said to him, "All your life God has been good to you, he gave you 73 years of life when you were only allowed 70. He gave you a wife, kids, a brand new SUV and a beautiful house, along with the many other blessings that you have experienced throughout your life."

To my amazement he said, "You are right! It took me 73 years and being on my dying bed to see God's blessings in my life."

Need I mention how shocked I was at his response?

Then in tears he said to me, "You know Malcolm, all my life, while I was rushing to go here and there, I was just rushing to get here. If I could have one more day, I would spend it in the backyard with family and friends.

After being here on my dying bed, I finally realized that everything that I have in this world is just for a moment, and now I would give anything just to have one more day."

As he had previously mentioned, by the same time, the following day, he was resting in peace. Many times we get lost in the offers of this world, not thinking that one day it will all be left behind. In the end, all that remains is the life you have lived and how you are remembered. Please take the time to thank God for the most wonderful gift anyone could ever ask for, LIFE. Always recognize the blessings He's bestowed upon you, through his love and mercy. Also, never forget to spend time with your family and loved ones.

The next time you are having a bad day, just remember, somewhere there is someone who would give anything just to have what you consider to be a bad day.

Today's Focus

- ❖ Each and everyday that we live we should make it our duty to spend it wisely.
- ❖ Take time to acknowledge the blessings in your life.
- ❖ It's ok to aim high, accomplish your goals and dreams but remember time should be set aside for your family and friends too.
- ❖ Don't wait for your dying days to seek God.
- ❖ Don't wait for your dying days to recognize the blessings given to you by God.

Reflection

- ❖ How do you spend your days?
- ❖ Do you take time to acknowledge the blessings in your life?
- ❖ Do you set aside time for family and friends?
- ❖ Do you have a relationship with God?
- ❖ How do you want to be remembered when you are gone?

Reflection

- How do you spend your days?
- Do you take time to acknowledge the blessings in your life?
- Do you set aside time for family and friends?
- Do you have a relationship with God?
- How do you want to be remembered when you are gone?

The Limit Is When You Say Stop™

Red Letter

Dear Reader,

By now you have transformed and finished reading this devotional with wonder of who I am. I'd like to say I'm your friend, but perhaps this is too soon. So let us settle for my first name, last name, and ephemeral life story.

I am Patrick Malcolm. I was born and raised in Jamaica West Indies by my single mother. As eldest and only son of three siblings, responsibility was instilled in me at an early age. The loss of my Father at 4 months old cemented this instillment and was an influential factor in how I matured as a child. It was difficult. Though, despite the absence of my father, I vowed to do whatever possible to provide guidance, be a provider and care-taker, for the sake of my mother and my family, then and now.

I have always had to work hard for everything I ever wanted, as I did not have the advantages that many other children had while growing up. Still, I always believed in my heart that one could do anything they set their mind to, if they only tried...and I did.

One could say my drive and determination has led to my profession as an Actor/Stuntman and Precision Driver. My appearances include various print magazines, commercials, and TV series such as *Law and Order* and HBO series *OZ* with stunt and precision driving performances in films such as *The Sorcerer's Apprentice, The Taking of Pelham 123,*

The Secret Life of Walter Mitty and *Batman*, to name a few.

My limit is not bound by what I do professionally. Helping those in need of advice, encouragement and/or a lending ear as a mentor is also a passion of mine and each opportunity I've encountered in life is an experience and testament which has helped me to write this book, along with my love for cars, which served as a great theme. My experiences have made me the strong, independent, positive, caring and giving person I am today and I can only hope after reading this book you will believe you are too. Remember, 'The sky is not the limit.' *The Limit is When You Say Stop.*™

Your Friend,

Patrick Malcolm

The Limit Is When You Say Stop™

Author's Note

If you love this book, do not hesitate to visit the following distributors below to show your support, provide feedback and share your review at:

AMAZON.com
AU-DE-CAN-US-UK
&
BARNES & NOBLE.com

———

Support via e-mail is welcomed at:
Makatree1@gmail.com

Also, do not hesitate to connect with us on:

 ❖ pejepublishing.com

If found, please return this book to:

❖NAME

❖PHONE

❖E-MAIL

Many thanks in advance for your kindness.

CPSIA information can be obtained at www.ICGtesting.com
Printed in the USA
BVOW030140130513
320520BV00002B/3/P